Life's Tragedies

By Dommageable and Mikey Shores

Table of Contents

Brain Smoothie

The Painter

No Handouts

That's a Wrap

Okay, I see you, go ahead then…

Le Repas

That's it

No Handouts (Snippet)

Didn't I tell you?

And you thought you could get rid of me?

Wait a minute

You hot and you know this

Sheeesh

ALL

DLC's Playlist

Life's Tragedies - Part 2

BRAIN SMOOTHIE

"I put the snake in the bag to flush down the toilet to save the soap from going in the trash. On the way to the restroom the kitchen set on fire and ablaze it went to the hospital and the nurse walked up to it and gave it a shot of cake in the tub with a spoon to let him know that everything was okay to be bored on a Wednesday night to be prepared for yesterday to be that person to go home on a game night just to be inconsiderate of what happens. Little did he know how to spell. A tree in the back yard was a cow who was not that old, but he fell in the tree in the front palace to see if he could follow along the same path to erase the fruit juice from the running microwave and that is it to be said." The cat cracked up.

THE PAINTER

PT 1

I pick the paint up, no need to flank us. Just push the weight up, no too much is dangerous. On a bus, on the way to work no fuss. Nobody but us, and when I say us, I mean me and my conscious running from a flock yelling trust. Tiptoe dip low. Sneaking around a mind like this, one step will make it blow. It's not too natural, it might be made up. But it comes to a halt and it's time to step off and I wish I never had dozed off.

PT 2

Next day I'm on the way to get new paint. This new picture will bring change and I mean cents. Like you thought it would be free but it's not. Wasting my time so that when I go my art will be worth more. Pshh, I'm like no, this was something invested and I'm really testing the new waters because unlike my father, I won't be stuck in or on a charter. Care for the need to explain why my trees are bending at the knees. Knowing that Febreze won't take the smell of paint from the breeze. Too much of the water that comes out the faucet a different color, one that is like no other. And then how is it I'm in the wrong place and the wrong time?

PT 3

I just needed groceries from the corner store, something that only I could afford. I didn't need anything more. I guess if I waited till tomorrow I would've left without the sorrow. But there won't be a tomorrow because it's my time at the wrong time. I just needed a few more minutes. My artwork was almost done but now it'll never be finished. Hopefully, somebody finds them and ill become famous like the greats. These young kids don't know the struggle or at least they think they do. Running up in my home like a bunch of hooligans. They were on a mission, nothing stopping them from killing, next thing you know I was looking down at my limp suit, bloodied up, there was nothing I could do. You see I knew it was a dream, but it really predicted the future. It might have not been me, but It could be...

"I'll be right back"

But you never did.

If you have an apple and you haven't eaten in days, do you eat it? No, you plant the seeds. See you're starving now, but after your investment, you'll never go hungry again. Easy right?

You can't be greedy.

You'll be just like them.

Don't question with "what ifs"

Think about their future, not just yours

How could you be so selfless but so selfish?

You know what, do what you got to do...

NO HANDOUTS

"Yeah, that's what I said last time, but now my pitches are all changeups."

"Oh really, I'm having a hard time recalling that. You look the same as when I saw you a while ago"

Drive. No reverse. Not quite in the spot correctly. Maybe if I turn the wheel to the right more, nope. Alright pull back out and turn left some then right. And…there we go. Easy, only took years. At least that's what if felt like. Now let me just slide out really quick. Oh, would you look at that, I'm on the line. Oh well, it will be fine, at least I got it in there.

'Well you see I might be in the same skin, but my mindset is different."

"Is that so. What makes you think you're different now?"

Wait, so you're telling me that I drank all the orange juice already? Wow, that's ridiculous man, you really need to learn how to pace yourself. Now, look at what you did. Looks like you have to go get more OJ kid. *Chop Chop*! Time is money or thirst; however, you want to view it. And while you're out don't forget to go to the office supply store and get the desk calendar you need. Note to self I guess.

"Then I don't know what to tell you, not much interest here, sorry."

"That s fine. Just to let you know, there is a shortcut."

What does she mean by that? We don't take shortcuts around

here unless it saves us money. Exactly. We are just going to forget she said that. Don't wait for me to tell you that you're in the red, because I never will. Petty right? Don't care it's my middle name. And there you are talking about a shortcut. Through what, to what? A sketchy alleyway where somebody will rob and harvest my kidneys, like really? But you know what we'll look into it to see how interesting it is. Hopefully, you're not wasting peoples time with this shortcut nonsense. It is crazy how I thought all of this through because it felt like it had been a few since the conversation had stopped.

"Alright about that shortcut, how and where can I find it?"

"It's where imagination and reality collide, and all you have to do is reach for it."

See I thought I was crazy at first, but now she is over talking in codes. What am I supposed to pull from that? I hate I even asked.

"Next time you should try making the waffles in the toaster I bought you last Christmas, John."

"Hey, it's not my fault my microwave works just as good, and why does it matter how it's cooked? It's going in than out"

"I don't think I needed to hear that last part."

"Well, you're the one complaining about my waffle making skills!"

"Take a chill pill John, and Mike give the man a break, he just got up from his wittle nap."

That's funny considering I tell that story every time. It's that story that dads tell each other when they're not talking about tools or sports and whatever else they stereotypically do. Luckily, I don't tell it every time, or it'd be repetitive, just saying. Like I have a list of stories I could pull up anytime for those moments but that's not the case. The case is that I bought a grill the other day for the house and forgot to get charcoal for the damn thing. Ridiculous right? I know. Not my fault though, Kate should've picked the kids up one that afternoon, but noooo. She was running late so I had to get them like you've got to be kidding me. *Too bad she had to tell me about the shortcut.* HA! There was something knocking away at us it seemed. Well then. It's time!

"Could you tell me why I got a call from your school today Johnny?"

"I don't know, you tell me."

You see my boy Johnny here is… quite the character. Teachers are always having a hard time with the kid. The thing is he's not doing anything wrong, except the idea of being taught. Like he is really stubborn, wants to know why he has to listen to a teacher when he can teach himself. I just want to point out to him at *the painting* I bought from the thrift store was made by someone who would love to take his place, considering he was dead. The poor guy was shot, the best dollar I've ever spent though!

"I just don't see why— "

"Why what? I should've just been homeschooled really, and this problem would've never occurred."

See what I'm talking about! The kids a real smart ass and that is the reason I got the call from the school. Dude needs to chill really because being this stubborn is not getting him anywhere.

THAT'S A WRAP

"And cut. Alright, that's a wrap for today."

Just getting started never departed from this *ship* after giving the *captain* nothing but lip. Wanted to watch the goodbyes from the tip as the ocean took the ship with a sip. Classified business is what we're on, who knew it'd take pretty long. All alone, I'm in the zone, I'll make it known, so watch ya tone. Too much of this and too little of that, how they done messed up and overlooked us. Taken from the bottom and placed on top like a cake topper, it's time to hop. Extinguish the fire that brought them here, non-stop till it's all clear.

It doesn't help to just rhyme things, make sure it has significance.

OKAY, I SEE YOU, GO AHEAD THEN...

Sea Boat. That was her name, it was more a trip down memory lane. But it came to a dead end with no gain. Trouble cornered you, but you found a way out. Now you make sure no one travels that route. Staying up late just to remember the date. No need to be blind to the cause, don't have to fixate. There was a flood and now it's time to compensate, it's now the time to appreciate the little boat that can inflate. Good thing you made it safely, wondering how the sinking boat didn't dip you in the gravy, now that's wavy. All of this for the *captain* to tell you it's too much going home. This *ship* has become a crowded nursing home. Full of people who have accepted their fate, now go ahead and open that gate.

LE REPAS

"It's not '86 anymore. All those lies you told can't be undone. All that killing makes you a murderer, so don't play innocent. Do you honestly know what your doing is fueling the fire? Now that you're strapped up and caught, do you have anything to say for yourself? Doesn't matter, kill him." (Detective 1)

Wait for it, it just might be that time for you to vanish. Because nobody wants you here still. Or we can just settle this the old fashion way and make sure nobody leaves here easily.

"Is there or will there be another time to bicker about the dispute some else time, perhaps tomorrow evening? I would hate to have to clean such a bloody mess at this time of day." (Detective 2)

"This is what I need to hear about, the patient you had here a week ago. If you would've let me know about him slash her, then this case could be done by now." (Detective 1)

"Puis-je utiliser les toilettes?"

"What? No bathroom breaks here bud. Answer my question first then you're free to go." (Detective 1)

"Je ne sais pas…"

"What do you mean "you don't know"? That's what guilty people say"

"J'ai un livre"

"A book about what? Please tell me it's something valuable…"

"Tragédies de la vie"

"Bet. Alright we're done here" (Detective 2)

THAT'S IT.

A cat, a green cat. Maybe a little yellow in the cat. But there was a cat. A small cat, one of those slick cats. A *tom*cat. Revised roughly cat. Jumped off the roof cat. Won't eat because it's never a hungry cat. Sitting still and waiting for the meal cat. Can't slip on ice type of cat. Laughing at nothing but a cat. Too many shoes to wear cat. A cat, a green cat. Maybe a little yellow in the cat. But there was a cat.

This and that call me Mr. Flapjack, a two stack, will keep you, them, occupied for now **halting them** from their long way down. Jumping in front of them but it was full of **clowns, like you**. He's there but with no explanation. We're here full of everything but **temptation.** Full off anything from his creation.

What is there to do?

All is left are a few…

There was something in the sink

What can I do to think?

Flip the book, hand the mic

Not on that hook, telling little *Tom*

I'm over here sitting real calm

You can come over here if you'd like

14

NO HANDOUTS (SNIPPET)

So, we are in real estate, and we are looking for a potential buyer. Someone who has the range to buy this type of house. It is unique and very attractive.

"What do you think Kate?"

"It is beautiful John"

DIDN'T I TELL YOU?

Killer I might be, these are the only eyes that I see. Put away the coffin, I just need a box. Dirt naps are good, especially because they take most out the hood. Or whatever people call it. Just when you thought it would fall in. All this weight brings the pressure, all this hate brings out the stretcher. So, bet what's up next? Bring out the check so I can stress. How much? There is no such… thing as a monster, but if they were real I'd be one. I'm talking mean, scary, ruthless and truth is we're just having fun. Play games and be ashamed, for the time you wasted so who are you hating? Who made you think you should be on the top shelf when you should be on the bottom. Quickly decide what's happening on a first serve base. Select all, because it's time to copy and replace it.

AND YOU THOUGHT YOU COULD GET RID OF ME?

Both enemies in the trenches see they're no eye to eye. Two tales from a lie. Waiting on no one, just to follow up with a cry. For help, but nobody's there. If it's not broken, then let it be. This was that and that was this, so pay the fee. That it costs to live and be free. I'm on the edge of the ledge with you. But you jumped the gun before I gave you something to do. Look around these objects are frozen and hung up with a clothespin. Blowing in the wind like those memories, and back to the trench with your enemy.

WAIT A MINUTE

Evil in thought, what is the problem? Causing destruction out of frustration. Muting the problems. What in tarnation?

What is it with you chickens? Like a duck is fly and you're here bobbin your neck. Like bruh, recognize the sanity that this chicken has jumping off the roof, trying to glide into the coup. Hens are falling feathers over beaks for the guy. How the perception is tainted by his small thinking capacity. For the little chicken that could.

So, you thought it was over, well it's not. We have a lot to discuss. How could it be that this son of mine be so reckless? Maybe it was all the late night munching I let him do as a kid. The real question is why I didn't take him to the doctor to get him checked out. It is clear as a sunny day and just as blinding because it has been a problem for him to understand he's the problem. You know? Anyway,

I'm done, I'll just ground him and that will be that.

YOU HOT AND YOU KNOW THIS

Cold morning it was. Minus the effort, the weatherman took to let us know. Here I am wearing shorts and a tank top to the bus stop. Just to let you know it's 30 degrees out here, yet I'm dressed like a college kid on spring break. How could I even end up in this situation? Teeth chattering and what not. This is gonna be the worst day ever. I would walk all the way home, but I might miss the bus. I'll take one chew out for today. Don't want to explain why I missed the bus and the reason for my bizarre attire today. So, looks like I'll just die of hyperthermia and frostbite or whatever. Maybe one of my friends will have an extra jacket. Hopefully. Goodness, how much longer am I gonna have to wait? Like, I have somewhere to be, so *chop chop*. This is why I hate taking the bus. Why can't my parents just drive me to school? Well since I'm going to die at any moment now, should I write a will? As a crystalized powdery figure lands on my nose. I knew I was in trouble now. Maybe I'm seeing things. And that wouldn't be any better. I hear a shout from behind, It's my neighbor Mrs. Steinworth.

"Do you need a ride to school Johnny?"

"Yes please," letting go the built-up stress in one exhale.

Mrs. Steinworth was an elderly lady, that was always doing yard work and walking her dog. With her short grey hair.

"Come on, you can't just do that!"

"Watch me," I told Jacob before hopping the fence to get my football. I was on my third football in less than a month. No way was I going to try and beg my parents for another one. I would not hear the end of it. "Okay Jacob, once I jump over be ready for me to toss the ball back over."

"Alright your funeral," Jacob said through his heavy breathing.

This wasn't just any old fence I was climbing over. It was the fence of an old man. They said he fought in a lot of wars and stuff. They also say he is really paranoid. Someone once told me he shot a dog without flinching. But hey, I needed the ball. Plus, I'm not scared of an old man! He can try and shoot me if his aim is as good as they say. Jacob was sweating a local community pool from the look of it. He wasn't even the one climbing the fence, what was he nervous for? I reached the top, pulled myself over, and dropped down with a thud. As I brushed myself off, I caught a glance of my ball. "I see it!" I yelled over at Jacob.

"Alright, whatcha waiting for? Grab it and toss it over!"

I took a look around. This grass looks decent for someone who rarely comes out of the house. Flowers right under his home. That's when I saw a dog house. I froze right then and there. My heartbeat felt like it was trying to jump out of my chest what happened next was even more terrifying. The sound of a chain clinking together. The noise of a snarl came shortly after. So, this was it. This is how I'm going to go. This dog is about to relieve me of my guts. It's going to be all over. I stood still like one the little green army men. I saw a shadow appear from the dome that kept the beast sheltered.

SHEEESH

You would think people were cool till they open their mouth without knowing what they are talking about. They'll come talk in your face and act like everything is fine. Fake is what they are. And to accuse me of stealing. Now your time is up dude. Don't ever accuse me of anything off a hunch.

Waiting for what? Someone to show up. To peel open and pour up. Poor luck more could suck. Wide open and more easy going. Buckle up to this piece of cake. Walk through my divided lake. In a pond, there is a snake. Tootles to them. Mickey Mouse is on to us. No clubhouse so we take the bus. Fill it to the line then let it overflow. Right onto the hand of the Sandman. Stealing sleep from you all, eyes so dry they evolve. Into statues looking straight ahead. To me to you. Who will wear this shoe? Dangerous by all means. Float right into the wall, through the ceiling they were rebuilding.

ALL

Is that all it takes? Is all that takes. All take, and Some take. All catches a break while Some get stuck. Mud pie or simple lie. All takes.

With no worries, All just takes. Regardless of feelings or your attitude. All will be your savior by securing your decision. All does this by not helping but making it worse. All takes with no regret, no when, no what, and no why. All has an All mentality. The one that makes you sick even when you're healthy as a sky that hasn't been tainted by All. Some taint the sky though, all has poisoned them. So, now Some go and pollute your lungs. All will take what's yours and more. From the shoelace in your sneakers to the hair on top of your head. All will brainwash you into thinking you're the problem when really it's Them. Them is All's henchmen. Them and They actually. They work the same as All, just with less power. All, Them & They, and Some. These are the world's killers.

DLC

Dangerous Love Cause

FIND ME

I'm just trying to get with Kehlani

Waiting for her to try and find me

On my way to the edge baby

And she's waiting, how crazy

And no, I won't hold back

Feel like I might just know that

Too much going holding onto you girl

As if I'm not gonna trip for you girl

But I'm just trying to get with Kehlani

Waiting for her to try and find me

Standing on top of the ledge baby

And she's fading, I'm crazy

Too late to hold back

Fell then and now I know that

Too much rolling holding onto you girl

As if I'm not gonna tip for you girl

But I'm just trying to get with Kehlani

Waiting for her to try and find me

BACKGROUND NOISE, TO YOU AT LEAST

I'm just trying to figure out how you think this is okay
Like Hold Up wasn't on its way, oh wait
Like two cups were enough for me
Like problems were a friend to me
Like chances done gave up on me
But I don't see why you, how you
Leave me hanging dry in the wind for you
Can't get a callback, no message that
You've moved on, that this, not your favorite song
That you're on your way to a different state
And so many things I say to show hate
For you, but it's a lie, because really
You're the reason why my boy Billy
Been watching from afar, like your favorite star
With a killer mentality waiting and ready,
To strike and spill what's steady
It's not the end of something good
But I'm the reason that you should
Pay close attention to me lately

Dommageable

KILLER CONFESSIONS

We took a soul while on the road
Never could I stop, it never glowed
Trying to be better that's The Show
Hard to keep composure
Probably the cost of all the exposure
How could you never notice?
That I'm due one…

Backstage tripping
Fast life gripping
Heart keeps ripping
Drink not spilling
Say I'm behind it all
This is worth living

But that's not the real story
There was never any real glory
It slipped from my hip
And all I could do was sip
I'm not the same anymore
No need to mask this lure
How could you never notice?
That I'm the one…

Backstage ripping
Fast life tripping
Heart keeps spilling
Drink not gripping

How I managed it all
This is worth killing

Jump into the street to figure it out
Instead of trying the pills now
In time I'll put the bottle down
Don't pick me up off the ground
*click

FINISH LINE

Ain't nobody speeding just to get to you

I dropped the bomb, now I'm late for curfew

I didn't come here just to get with you

I might be tired but I ain't dead yet

I might be unlucky but how better can it get

My life lessons will put yours in question

Now we're kicking down those doors

Never was I done, I want more

I'm about to step in the wrong direction

Don't get stuck begging for a reflection

All these people and you're worried about him?

All these equals but I'm the special gem

Quit making excuses I'm about to lose it

You wait crying for something unreal

My plate is dying for some fresh kill

So how about I hook you tonight

Dommageable

And then you'll become my favorite meal
We waited for it, so now they come
Those moments when you wanted some
I'm all out should've asked earlier
Stop trying to be just like that girl
You waited till the middle of the night
To call ya boy that's off that smite
Gotta be crazy if I can't do you right
But ain't nobody speeding just to get to you

THAT TIME

I feel like it's the early 2000's
Back when I had no power
My dirty eyes need a shower
I kill my pain with this tower…
Of liquor, I'd like to think I'd miss her
Can't catch any fish but I'm a fisher
So, what you mean that there's plenty
What you mean you can't see me
I'm stuck on you but I wanna be free
It's like you got a part of me…
But eventually, it'll be clear you see
I think it was meant to be…
But this vision got lost in murky water
I just got up trying to fall for her
This is me and only me

I'll give it up when I'm released
I hate to live this life so displeased

LIFE'S TRAGEDIES PART 2

Memoir

By Dommageable

I can't give you all of me

I got all these problems right in front of me

Just because you love me, you ain't saving me

- Lou Val

LIFE'S TRAGEDIES

What you gonna do, drink away the pain?
Shit, I'm like maybe
I done had two cups and true enough
It might not sound that crazy
So, what you want ain't real?
Huh, I really thought so
I roll my windows up cause I rolled one
Thump it in the solo cup, yeah the red one
It was full of liquor but now it's all gone
The life that I live feels like acid love
Tripped on a sidewalk, fell into a tight hug
Python grip rolled into a gold rug
Not much, but it was hard for me to budge
I don't need shit but a new pair of lungs
Probably a liver too
Because that shit is really muddy
It was like quicksand and the liquor got lovey-dovey
Holding me back, but expressed my true feelings
Cause me sober is like screaming in an empty building
But then here comes a crash
Shouldn't have tried to do the dash
Awaken from this coma
To see the life I really had
But really, I just need a glad trash bag
To throw away the emotion called sadness
I'm really happy that I had this

Dommageable

And the thing is I never awoke

I was dressed in the grim reapers cloak

Because my soul could never float

How you late to your own death?

I was probably partying with what I had left

Drugs on the table and the scythe is what I kept

Played him in his own game, put in what I felt

That was nothing, and the dreams got swept

That's when I picked up the life taker and slashed through his chest

Freed up all the ghosts that never slept

Just to come back to reality for my people who never wept

Life's Tragedies

We meet at the same place every day. That being the bed we sleep in. Waking up, hitting the snooze button and then going back into a deep slumber. Until the ringing sound of the alarm clouds our head again. We get up, put our slippers on and then go off to the bathroom. Depending on what our stomach feels like, our number 1 can turn into a number 2. Number 2 always makes us run late. So, we try to avoid those. We wash our hands, then brush our teeth. Clothes already picked out and ready for us to put on. That shirt with those shorts, and those socks as well. I'm still in my slippers because all my shoes are ending up in my trunk. And when I say slippers, I mean Nike sandals. I close the... I mean we close the garage as the outside air smacks us in the face as if we did something wrong. I throw my bag into the car then open the trunk, our shoes have to match our outfit. We make the switch and get into the car. We take off the emergency brake, start the car up, and head off.

We walk on the stage as one, but when the show is done its only you. For about an hour or two, time moves fast on top of that platform. Each verse hyping the crowd up more and more. You can tell who you're dedicated fans are. Because you sing all the songs, mainstream, and lowkey. Speakers look as if the devil himself is using souls to scratch through. We can barely hear. And that is when we start to pull apart. Now you take the stage and the mic. Single-handed, you take the crowds attention to a whole new level to the point where I ask, "where was all this noise when we were playing together?" Two skips...

Just like that, it's over. No warning, time to be an adult. In a world that is not prepared for me, but damaged. Not able to function properly without my aid. To boring without my touch. This is what we have waited for so long yet dread the day it has come. Why not be able to wait longer. Why must I be rushed into this life I'm not ready for. There is no class for this, just the idea of being content with what you choose or get. Let this show that from now until the end of days that we are finished.

Part?

Doesn't matter how much time is taken from me, just know you're more than a movie scene. Don't say I never tried, I could never lie, my hands were always tied. All of this for you to let go? Was there something I'm supposed to know? I'm done celebrating a year of getting closer to death, look at the mirror this is all that's left.

PART 0

How is it that people can be so irresponsible? Never did they stop to see if it was possible. You can get played and then better yourself. But you never got to experience life itself. And for that, I cannot put you to blame. But how can you leave you first life unclaimed? How could you fall for someone out of line? You end up moving fast, how did not see it wouldn't last? Why would you ruin y(our) time?

PART 13

Never did I see it happening. You talked to me to only go and block me. The first connection I ever had. That's when I knew I need you bad. No matter who would step in between, I was always there, your only fiend. And no matter who you were acquiring, the kid was always conspiring. Only when I finally get you it falls apart. Our connection will always be my favorite art. Never could I let you go, you know you'll always be my first snow.

PART 8

How could they leave now? Will they ever come and get you? They leave me with no communication, seems like I was left without any hesitation. Is that what I am? A pawn, an object for you to use as leverage? Always knew I was never wanted, and that was the start of a life so daunting.

PART 6

How could I be going with someone I never knew, maybe it's been so long since you came through. My memory was hazy, but maybe my patience has become too lazy. You see I know everyone around you, but how come I've never seen you? She says your spending time with him, yet that summer I barely saw him. Don't lie to me.

PART 7 – SECTION 2

They say if it happens once it'll happen twice. Something like history repeats itself. How come you tell me these are important, that must have been to some extent. I've been ready to go but it looks like you're a no show. The first change I noticed, the first time I became hopeless. Don't cry to me.

PART 16

I see why they never say goodbye. Because when people say they'll be back, they better mean it. I guess that has lost meaning too. The person I barely knew had jinxed himself, his life no longer itself. Telling me after some long commotion, that if his heart no longer in motion, that they would finish the notion. Both left me by choice. And they wonder where's my remorse. Don't die on me.

PART 7 – SECTION 1

How dare tear me away and then end up leaving me astray. Is this what you intended because there is no way this plan can be implemented. This was going so well, I hope you wish you never fell. Don't make me see.

PART 20

Please don't talk to me. People neglect me too easy. I'm okay as always, me being happy will always be a faze

PART 15

Leaving me here, never letting me go anywhere. Don't introduce me to your new fling, none will ever be a thing. How come everything is my fault? Nobody ever comes here so why strike me over a small spot. Chipped teeth never matter to you, only coming back to make me look like a fool. Days spent doing nothing but talking to myself, mentally falling apart because there was no who could help. Don't try with me.

PART 14

This is what it's like to live with evil. Saying I'll never be anything but a copy of him, not even a sequel. Telling me I'm no good and worthless as ever. That me being great would always be a never. Driving me to hate myself, why am I here? This would be the last time I shed a real tear.

PART 18

No loops needed for this one. You see she was different. I saw that there was potential. Now I tested the waters seeing what she could take. Why is it that the things you need come too late? She was too young, but I always wanted things I couldn't have. There was no way I had a chance, there were too many complications. Now I don't fall easy, so it took time. Seeing her every chance I had, mostly every other day. I made small moves to finally talk to her. I knew it was real. But leave it to me to get greedy, I needed more. Why would I rush someone who shows care for me? On my mind all the time, when I was with and without her. Loving all of our little dates. And now I see you now and then, hoping you won't leave me like everyone else has. It hurts to know this will end eventually. I hate to be in love with something I can't have.

PART 17

Back at this again, trying to find something I'll hopefully win. I tried to force something that wasn't there. But all she had to do was be clear. No matter what I did and what I gave, she still couldn't be obtained. She took a great deal out of me and I was still left lonely.

PART 19

She needed emotions I didn't have, but we all know why. I guess she didn't know she was emotionless herself. How come after I tell you so much, you decide to let me go. The same as everyone else I know. So selfless but yet a little selfish. She didn't give me enough time, yet why would I trap a free bird? That took what was left, that shook my soul from the shelf.

Trap 18

Why be upset you're not invited, when you've never tried this. Don't come at me sideways when you've never come to my ways. I'll tell you that it's your fault, but you knew that anyway. Just don't leave them as you left me. You still come regardless.

Trap 17

Damn, in a cab again as usual. Never was it fair, but this is ridiculous and could have been avoided. How can I have fun with no way out, shunned? That's all right, I'll find my own way out.

Trap 16

Why today? This month will never be the same. No celebrations this year… and the next. Because after that day I knew the end was near.

Dommageable

And I didn't even cry.

Not one bit. Nothing could cause my eyes to water except a windy day, dust, or maybe cutting some onions. I would say my acting skills are on point. But when does the acting become lying? I find myself holding back on sharing information because I don't want to share too much. Nobody needs to know. They'll either feel sorry for you, basically pity, or you'll be judged by what you may never become. Never would I say something about someone that diminishes their character; I know I wouldn't want somebody to say something awful about me. That's when I came up with a great solution. Since they need emotions then fake them. You can't feel anything, and you start to realize why do anything? Don't need someone's help, don't need someone to talk to. We need time back, all the wasted time spent chasing things you can't have. Dreams that'll never be because you don't know where to start. People that come and go so quick that you lose count. And all you can do is sit there and doubt. More times than ever has life counted us out. Never were we to see what a normal... no, a fair life is about. You can't believe yourself. It's easy to fake being what the eyes can see but what the mind can't comprehend. I will always wonder why I am always looking at a dead end. They never wanted to see you grow, there was never any potential. You're on top but the roof is missing, and you'll keep falling because you never had a beginning. When there is nowhere to go, you circle. Sitting here trying to figure out why I am doing the same thing every day. Sometimes I don't even know why I would care about anything. They keep talking to someone with no emotion, yet they'll never know my brain is in a commotion. I've been battling myself.

When the drinking and drugs make you realize. Is this what I am? No one. Why do I associate with these people? Are these my friends? This is not even my crowd, but I'm here. I should just leave, but I feel stuck. People complain about everything and can never be grateful. I know when I look in the mirror that I can never believe I'm still pushing. You see, I know I'm the worse person alive, I don't have to be told that. I try my hardest, but the energy of having to keep up an appearance Is overwhelming. As soon as you forgot to smile, then the mood becomes rebellious. And with that, I can never be my true self; whatever that is.

I know when you read this you'll try to understand, and you won't. Every time she's a replica of you. Have you ever chased the best feeling you ever had? I imagine that is what fiend feels like. Maybe I might be one for you. It seems silly to be so. It's just that when I thought it was done for, you came and plucked my life up. Late night messages on a school night. Never would our conversations be boring, and never could I forget you. And that's probably why they all resemble you. The original life taker is what I concluded, but I'd rather be high off you then live this sober without. But we're not worried about a DLC, because there's nobody but me, and I've been rolling deep.

I've done it all and seen it all without being here too long. So, you can let go now.

But I can't, not that I'm worried about being missed. No, forget that. Too many people counting on me with no help.

And you knew how I felt. You know how I feel, I don't. They can explain what it means, and why it's important, but unfortunately, I stopped listening long ago.

And they will come and go like the time does. I just can't believe it's going this fast. It doesn't need to slow down though. While you're reading this right now, let's talk about something important. As time has passed me by I've learned many things. One of the biggest ones is to not worry about things that are out of your control. If you can't change the outcome after exhausting the possibilities, you should put it on the back burner. Trust me, if I knew my life would end up like this, I would have focused on it more. And now it's too late for such a thing. Unable to kill what is already dead, but rather it's beaten out of existence. That's how this feels. Tell me what can I do?

I'm not your stunt double.

Dommageable

Ha. It'll never be over. Till I say it is.

You can tell me how it is, or don't. Will it matter anyway? When they always need this for that and barely know the facts. I'm trying to tell you where I'm really heading. Now listen. The ship has already sailed so there's no turning back on this one-way trip. For every person you meet, there seems to be someone just like them not too far away. Except this ship doesn't have a return date.

*Click

Voicemail starts to play:

"Aye yo bro what's going on? Man, I was out of it today. *There is a quick pause and sigh.* Anyway, I was just gonna say... I don't even know where to start. Thank you. I mean it, I know I haven't been the best of friends lately but I'm sorry. I mean it this time. Like seriously, too much is going on right now, I just don't know what to do. I figured you'd be sleep and not pick up your phone, typical you ha-ha. *Mumbling about something.* I guess I called you to tell you that I'm tired as fuck, of everything. Bro, remember as kids we said we'll write a book or some shit? Yeah, man, we need to follow through with that in all seriousness bro. Yeahh, well I'll see you sometime. Alright bye.

And that was the last time I heard from you. I wonder if somehow you were given a chance that you'd still be here. You were so smart; how could this happen to you? I wish I could've seen some type of sign or something. I'm sorry this took so long but you don't know how hard it is to do this without you. I don't even know what to call this thing we made, but I'm sure everyone will like it. Thank you.

Made in the USA
Lexington, KY
02 September 2019